Beautiful
Northern Nevada

"Learn about America in a beautiful way."

Beautiful
Northern Nevada

Concept and Design: Robert D. Shangle
Text: Paul M. Lewis

First Printing May, 1981
Published by Beautiful America Publishing Company
P.O. Box 608, Beaverton, Oregon 97075
Robert D. Shangle, Publisher

Library of Congress Cataloging in Publication Data
Beautiful Northern Nevada
1. Nevada—Description and travel—1951—Views. Lewis, Paul M.
F842.L48   917.93'0022'2   81-7746
ISBN 0-89802-101-4   AACR2
ISBN 0-89802-100-6 (pbk.)

Photo Credits

JAMES BLANK—*page 17, page 21, page 27, page 28, page 36, page 37, page 42, page 44, page 47, page 51, page 55, pages 56-57, page 58, page 61.*

STEVE TERRILL—*page 18, page 19, page 20, page 22, page 23, pages 24-25, page 26, page 29, page 30, page 31, page 32, page 33, page 34, page 35, page 38, page 39, pages 40-41, page 43, page 45, page 46, page 48, page 49, page 50, page 52, page 53, page 54, page 59, page 60, page 62, page 63, page 64.*

**Color Separations and Printing
by
Universal Color Corporation
Beaverton, Oregon**

Contents

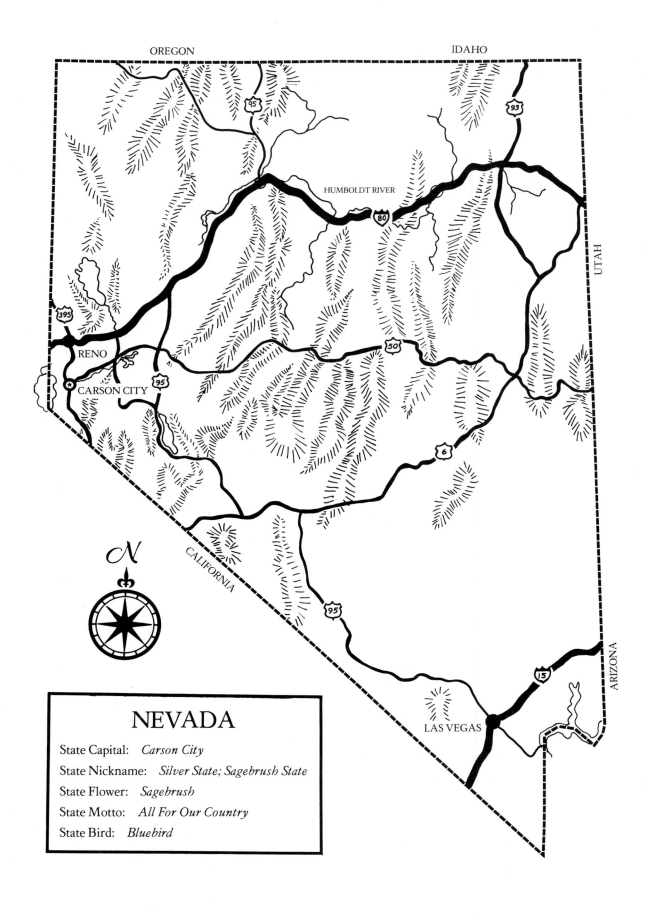

OREGON

IDAHO

UTAH

ARIZONA

CALIFORNIA

95

93

HUMBOLDT RIVER

80

395

50

RENO

CARSON CITY

95

6

95

15

LAS VEGAS

𝒩

NEVADA

State Capital: *Carson City*

State Nickname: *Silver State; Sagebrush State*

State Flower: *Sagebrush*

State Motto: *All For Our Country*

State Bird: *Bluebird*

Introduction

Nevada is still a state of mystery to many people who don't live in and even to some who do. So, even in this age of enlightenment, the state's image has suffered from the pronouncements of those instant experts whose usual capsule comment on Nevada goes something like this: "Well, after Reno and Las Vegas, what is there?" Even residents of bordering regions seem to have a kind of "wrong-headed" fixation about the Silver State. They often travel to and through parts of it, headed for the gambling and night spots of Reno, Vegas, and a few other towns.

Most of Nevada is part of the Great Basin country. That situation, combined with a generally sparse rainfall, has produced some extensive deserts. But these arid stretches are far from unrelieved sandy wastes. Nevada's face is wrinkled with range after range of north-south mountains, especially in the north, west, and center. Even a corner of the high and mighty Sierra intrudes into the western edge.

Nevada is among the bigger of the king-sized western states. If its corrugated surface were spread out flat, it might cover all the states around it and Texas, too. Even without the up-and-down dimensions, there are a lot of square miles to be counted: 110,690 of them. Those mountains are not only numerous, some of them are very tall—more than 13,000 feet. Many of them are barren, with soils that glow under Nevada's sun with brilliant colors of the mineral treasures within them. Others, such as the tall Ruby Range southeast of Elko, have, occasionally, thick stands of pine, aspen, and mountain mahogany. Nevada's mountain and valley meadows are the glory of the world in the spring and summer. Wild iris crowd into a dense, blue cloak on the slopes; gaudy cactus flowers color the desert floor. Blue lupine and orange-red Indian paintbrush, growing by mountain trails, drink the waters of melting snowcaps on the ridges and peaks.

Some of that mountain melt goes to feed the rivers and creeks that nourish the valleys and even parts of the deserts. Many of these streams are only part-time workers; their beds become dry washes in late summer and fall. But a few of them are big enough to put in a full shift. The Humboldt is Nevada's boss river. Its route, from east to west across northern Nevada, is closely related to the history of the region,

Indian and pioneer. The Humboldt was an important access river to the West during the early explorations and during the great westward movement that developed in the middle and later years of the 19th century. Three other major streams are found in the west-central corner, which the Humboldt aims for but never quite reaches. All three—the Carson, Walker, and Truckee—rise on the east slope of the Sierra in California. Like most Nevada streams, none of these four ever gets to go ocean-voyaging. Their waters either flow into Nevada lakes with no outlet or disappear into alkali sinks in the desert.

One of the lakes involved is the instant kind—Lahontan Reservoir, behind Lahontan Dam, and which receives the waters of the Carson. But the other two are long-time residents. Big and beautiful Pyramid and Walker lakes are fed by the Truckee and Walker rivers, respectively. These two lakes are leftovers from the late, great Lake Lahontan, which sat on most of northwestern Nevada when the world was newer. The third big body of water, partly in western Nevada and partly in California, is Lake Tahoe, in an idyllic forested setting high up on the eastern flank of the Sierra and famous for its showy green-blue tint and 1,776-foot depth.

This book, in both a pictorial and textual sense, is concerned with the parts of Nevada outside of the southern corner dominated by Nevada's biggest city. The Las Vegas area is a separate story, told by a separate volume in the Beautiful America series. Southern Nevada and its glittery city have the heavy end of Nevada's light population. But the big spaces of the state—the north, the west, and the center—are all the more fascinating because they are still, in this era of togetherness, mainly unpeopled. That's a lot of space dedicated to something other than the human race. Most of it is little changed except by the natural evolution of the earth.

Nevada's largely pristine landscape may be very nearly unique among the states south of Alaska and east of Hawaii. Nevada is one of the smallest states in population and one of the biggest in area. So it has a right to its empty spaces. The Reno and Vegas areas have the lion's share of Nevada's half-million persons. A handful of other sizeable towns in the interior contribute, perhaps, another 40 or 50 thousand of the state's highly individualistic, independent, resourceful individuals.

Until about the midpoint of this century, Nevadans had been content to let their state remain a mystery. Courteous and hospitable toward visitors, they were unwilling to blow their own horn to cash in on the tourist business. That, of course, changed with the advent of Las Vegas and Reno as gambling and entertainment centers. Now, with competition for the gambling dollar coming from East Coast states, these revenues may be leveling off for Nevada. So heavy promotion of the "outback" may be part of the future.

The history of western civilization in Nevada begins with Mormon settlements and mining camps. The famed Comstock Lode of the Virginia Range in Nevada's middle-western corner energized the formation of territory and state. When Nevada was the western part of Utah Territory in the mid-1800s, Brigham Young, the Territorial governor, sent out traders along the Humboldt and Carson valleys, one of the first being Ragtown by the Carson River. Another, known as Mormon Station and later Genoa, was established as a livestock corral in the Sierra foothills. Genoa is still in existence, still a tiny community, and oldest town in the state.

The forty-niners used the Humboldt Road too, mainly as a route to the California gold fields. A decade later, the rush to the western slope of the Sierra was reversed when silver deposits of enormous value were discovered in the Washoe region of western Nevada. The richest and most famous of the silver discoveries was the Comstock Lode, making the name of Virginia City internationally celebrated and spawning countless romantic legends of the wild, chaotic, and wicked mining camps. The stories of people swarming all over the place, staking claims and fending off the passel of hoodlums, rowdies, and outright crooks who had arrived with the swarm looking for easy pickings, was endless. The tales of Mark Twain in *Roughing It* came out of his two years on the Comstock diggings. Other chroniclers of the time were drawn to the Virginia camps, expert storytellers like Dan de Quille (William Wright), the Nevada writer whose *The Big Bonanza* is regarded as the best of the books on Comstock mining camp life.

After Nevada became a Territory in its own right in 1861, things began to settle down and the mining camps of the Comstock—Virginia City, Silver City, Gold Hill, and such—became more stable communities with a sizeable industrial base and a determined squelching of the wilder aspects of mining camp life. The boom ended in the 1880s and the population of the Virginia Range towns dropped off. Small spurts of silver ore production have brought from time to time renewed interest in large-scale silver and gold mining operations. But that aspect of Nevada economics has gradually subsided to the point where it has lost any real importance.

The gentler fascinations of Nevada are really only beginning to be appreciated. The flashier side of the state's history and development have overshadowed them for too long. Plant life, wild life, long vistas, brilliant mountainscapes, and enormous canyons acquire more visibility in the world of humankind as they come out from behind the glint of precious metal, whether those riches be extracted from the ground or raked in from the gaming table. We hope you'll be able to take an armchair wander through a land that is as unspoiled and enchanting as any place on earth.

P.M.L.

The Humboldt Valley

Northern Nevada is the domain of the Humboldt, which winds across the greater part of this varied region. One of the two big interstate highways in the state follows the twists and turns of Nevada's biggest river, from its beginnings in the east to the sink that blots up the ragged remains of the stream in the west. The Humboldt begins and ends in Nevada. The interstate, I-80, of course, does not. Before and after its 400-mile odyssey across this empty land, I-80 is in business elsewhere. But surely in no other place does the highway encounter the Oz-like changes of scenery and weather that it does in the Nevada stretches.

Before the road was a four-lane freeway, it was US Highway 40, a famous and familiar transcontinental passage, which for many years, was traveled by millions of latter-day explorers motoring along the wide-open spaces of the West. Still farther back in time, the Humboldt road was already a well-worn pathway, practically a parade route for the panting armies of determined goldseekers marching wild-eyed to the Mother Lode. The river route was tortuous, but relatively safe. Only at the western end, where the rivers vanished into sinks and the harsh desert opened up, did the unprepared, ill-advised, and over confident emigrants fail to survive the journey.

Today's superhighway, in the manner of superhighways everywhere, tends to insulate the traveler from his surroundings. The feeling of detachment peculiar to today's traveler is only illusory, of course. Two thousand pounds of automobile is like a little house on wheels, and a smooth, broad highway like the floor of that house. But just over the edge, the rugged country of northern Nevada is as elemental and unforgiving as it ever was. The only obvious change is that the Paiutes and other local tribes have made an accommodation with the invaders of their lands and do not annoy today's motorized caravans.

The Humboldt rises in the northeast Nevada mountains, up near the corner. Today, travelers coming into the state from northern Utah zip across the border after passing through what was a fearsome barrier to the wagon trains of a mere hundred years ago—the Great Salt Lake Desert. Some of those emigrants avoided the peril by taking a northern detour around it and coming south, through what is now the extreme northeast corner of Nevada. This early trail was for a while the overland mail route, along Goose Creek into the Thousand Springs area, so named by pioneer travelers who found water there.

Montello, Oasis, and Wells are names on the map in this area. The first two are tiny way stations not far from the border. Wells is a major crossroads and railroad town farther inside the state. It has around one thousand inhabitants. US Highway 93 crosses here on its north-south journey through the long eastern side of Nevada. Since the latter years of the 19th century, the town has been a supply point for cattlemen of the upper Humboldt and the eastern valleys of the Ruby Range. Wells is also the northeastern gateway to those tall mountains, whose summits may wear patches of snow all summer. The Rubys are Nevada's ''Alps'' and favorites of deer hunters.

On the western side of the range are roads to and through the Ruby Range, from nearby Deeth and Halleck and from Elko, farther down the Humboldt Valley. One of these routes, State Highway 11, crosses the valley at the north end of the range that divides the Rubys from the East Humboldt Mountains. This low spot has the distinction of being one of the country's coldest spots in the winter, made so by frigid blasts that sweep in over northern Nevada from Idaho. The icy winds slam into the tall Rubys, making a minus 50-degree deep freeze of the defiles as their paralyzing breath piles cold upon cold.

On the way across the mountain pass, the road encounters Secret Canyon, a narrow chasm of Secret Creek. The creek waters a little hidden Shangri-la higher up called, naturally, Secret Valley. This green mountain meadow was formerly a handy retreat for Indians fresh from a raiding party and even for cattle rustlers. The state road crosses Secret Pass and descends to Ruby Valley on the eastern side. The lower elevations of the mountains and the eastern valley are thick with deer, when colder weather and snow forces them to come down from the heights.

The side roads from Elko do a thorough job of investigating the western flanks of the Rubys. Elko itself is well worth an investigation. It is the big town around these parts, the main crossroads of eastern Nevada's cattle country. Elko is an advance camp for the hunters and fishermen who fan out from it in all directions into the mountain· and valley wilds of a great empty area bigger than some states. Elko's population of around 8,000 makes it the biggest town between Salt Lake City and Reno-Sparks, a fitting distinction for the seat of giant Elko County, which is by itself all of northeast Nevada.

Like a lot of western communities, Elko started as a railroad shipping center, serving the nearby mining districts and the pioneer farms in the valleys running alongside the Ruby Mountains. By 1869 it was a town in more than name and its early years were characteristically on the wild side. Though it never became all decorum and manners, Elko settled down after a while to the point where the saloons were not the only locales for social events. After the mining boom was over, Elko prospered as the capital of the rangelands, celebrating its rise to eminence by building an Opera Hall in the late 1870s, where traveling companies brought their entertainments.

A big loop road, partly paved, strikes into the Rubys from Elko. The road runs along the mountains' west side, crosses high Harrison Pass (7,247 feet) and skitters up Ruby Valley on the east. Just out of town the route reaches a high point on the nearby hills, where a broad view of the community and its valley is a splendid treat, day or night. Side roads climb up the slopes from the main route farther down the valley, following the sparkling mountain streams that meander down from the higher levels. Lamoille Creek is one of these, bedded in a glacier-cut canyon where groves of aspen, willow, and pine leave space for abundant wildflowers. This is granite country, with veins of minerals containing beautiful and valuable gem stones.

One of the most attractive of Nevada camping facilities is in Thomas Canyon, nearby. In a bowl formed by the high surrounding peaks, the camp is also close to a dramatic waterfall and, in season, a meadow full of mountain flowers. Still farther up the mountain, a forest road ascends into a wonderland of brilliant wildflowers in summer. The Ruby Mountains are well endowed with lakes, too. Several of them are reached farther ahead on this same trail. The lakes vary from shallow to deep, pristine fishing waters where such is permitted. Lying on both sides of the summit, some of them are so high on the mountain they never lose all of their icy coating during the summer. The highest point is reached at Ruby Dome—11,349 feet. Reaching it is a worthwhile endeavor, if just for the panorama of earthly glories that opens to those who make the effort.

There is a town called Jiggs farther south in the valley below the mountains. Another trail up the slope from Jiggs reaches a lake at 9,000 feet. A few miles south of Jiggs is the road to Harrison Pass across the Rubys. The route is along a flashing stream flanked by lovely mountain meadows. The pass is at 7,247 feet and from it there is another ''spy-in-the-sky'' view that goes beyond description. This one includes Ruby Valley and the long line of Nevada's eastern border mountains.

Carlin is 23 miles west on the Humboldt Road, or Interstate Highway 80, to keep things current. It is another of the river stations that figured so prominently on the Overland Trail to California. Providing thirsty travelers with liquid assets was, and still is, an important function of this railroad town, where visitors to this lonely landscape traditionally have been refreshed and revived.

North of the Elko-Carlin neighborhood, there is still a lot of Nevada, featuring some good-sized mountains and one officially designated wilderness. State Highway 51 from Elko winds through it. By the time the road reaches Owyhee in the Duck Valley Indian Reservation near the Idaho border, the mileage reads nearly one hundred. A few connecting routes, paved or not, also explore the region. State Highway 11 branches west from the primary route after 27 miles, by climbing into the sagebrush and grass-covered ridges of the Independence Range. From Lone Mountain, the high point here, the long look west, if the air is clear enough, is reward enough for climbing a four-mile trail to the summit. The experience must be something like that of Cortez, ''Silent upon a peak in Darien,'' when he beheld the Pacific Ocean. The wrinkled carpet of the earth unrolls to the dim and distant horizon, across the wide, fierce Black Rock Desert to the Cascade foothills, a hazy purple on the edge of the world. Faint patches on the southwest horizon are the Humboldt and Carson sinks. The raw angularity of the land tells the story of its restless movement during many titanic upheavals throughout the ages.

Close by in the Tuscarora hills, gold and silver mining still goes on. This high mining town at 6,200 feet was a swinger during the frenzied boom times of the 1870s and 1880s. Tuscarora had a rough, tough reputation in those days as the leading community in a district on the Tuscarora Mountains. Now its population is little more than a handful, but for a time, during the town's golden—and silver— days, several thousand persons called it home. Though the more savage elements in the district made the name of Tuscarora synonymous with the wildest of the mining West, the majority of citizens were content with the more sober pastimes.

Between Tuscarora and the nearby Independence Range on the east are cattle ranches and rangelands, scattered through the long valley that reaches south to the Great Basin and north toward Idaho. It is at this point that Nevada ceases to be a part of the Great Basin, where stream drainage is to the north and into the Snake River in Idaho. The Independence Mountains have more sagebrush than timber but are no less striking for that. Their peaks are ordinarily covered with snow all the year, and their canyons provide the water for groves of mountain aspen. The snowfields are bordered in summer with multicolored carpets of wildflowers. Secluded and narrow Jack Creek Canyon is especially noteworthy, and here the Forest Service has established a small number of campsites.

The pass over the range at this point produces as many sumptuous panoramas as Lone Mountain's summit. The desert mountain ranges of Nevada swim into view, taking on decorator hues in the slanting sunlight. The purple mountain majesties are again on the far horizon, blending into sapphire and dark blue-red; nearer ridges show up in a warm reddish brown.

As the west-slope road continues in the direction of Owyhee, it comes into the broad, dissected valley of the Owyhee River South Fork, where the deer and the antelope (and even wild horses) roam over a seemingly limitless playground. The main road from Elko heads along the eastern side of the range. Another part of the journey is through the upper valley of the Humboldt North Fork, biggest of that river's tributaries and one of the most northerly of the south-flowing streams. At the approximate divide between the north-and south-flowing drainage, a gravel road climbs over some low ridges to the east for 21 miles and reaches north into the area of the Jarbidge Wilderness.

Jarbidge is another illustrious name in the annals of Nevada mining. The town is still a going concern after having been a gold camp in this exceptionally rugged corner of the Humboldt National Forest. The odd-sounding name, Jarbidge, is an adaptation of an Indian expression for the Devil, descriptive enough of this primeval mountainscape with its supply of hot springs. The Jarbidge Range is also one of the most heavily timbered parts of Nevada.

Charleston, possibly the titleholder for the wildest and most lawless mining camp in the whole state, has disappeared after a career of distinguished mayhem that lasted well into this century. The road into this area is open only in the gentler seasons. It passes the little valley where the old town was. The summit of Copper Mountain is reached on a one-mile trail from the road. At a 9,912 feet altitude, it opens up another of those breath-catching views of raw, tumbled earth that Nevada specializes in. This time a highly placed explorer can look north into the fearsome Idaho Sawtooth Mountains and their sumptuous gorges.

Flashing streams depart from the Jarbidge Wilderness heights to northern points through narrow canyons. The Bruneau River is one of these, a fishing stream of high repute. So are the Jarbidge River, Coon Creek, Bear Creek, and a multitude of other streams, where trout are in such abundance that it all seems as if the earth has just been created. This primitive range still has the ''just-new'' look that is becoming rare in a world where man has changed so much of nature in some way. The Jarbidge mining district, once the main producer of gold in Nevada, still yields up gold ore. The real treasure is this isolated region itself, a natural paradise that makes Nevada rich beyond measure.

About midway across northern Nevada on the route of the Humboldt is another of those small communities, which on first inspection seem likely to close up any day and retire from the world. But Battle Mountain is important to the economy of the area around it, beyond any mere consideration of size. Nevada is still very much a mining state and in all directions around the town the mines are in active operation.

Two railroads, the Southern Pacific and the Western Pacific, bring in a major part of Battle Mountain's provisions and take out the yield of the mines and ranches. The town's name is borrowed from an actual mountain to the south, which was the scene of skirmishes between Indians and settlers. Though the Battle Mountain mining district existed during the boom times, the town has always kept a low profile. Despite its warlike name, Battle Mountain has gone light on the fighting and stayed pretty much to its diggings. Maybe that has been one reason for its steady production well into this century, a long career outlasting most.

The Humboldt River takes tentative aim at Nevada's northwest corner in another 40 miles or so, but executes, instead, a sharp turn to the southwest, for the home stretch to its vanishing point in the Black Rock Desert. Just at the bend the river is replenished by the Little Humboldt, a ''sometime-stream'' out of the Santa Rosa Range to the north. Here is the biggest town along the river after Elko. Winnemucca counts about 3,500 in her population. The town was started by a Frenchman in 1850 as a trading post on the Overland Trail, and was known first as French Ford, then as French Bridge (in 1865). The settlement was a river crossing point on the Trail, first a ford and then with a bridge.

Winnemucca received its name of record when the railroad tracks reached its valley site in 1868. The station was named for the wise old Paiute chieftain, Winnemucca, who fought the white man's encroachments while at the same time seeking peace with the invaders. Ore shipping became the town's primary business, then livestock shipping when silver prices dropped. Winnemucca got big and blustery enough by 1873 to take the Humboldt County seat away from Unionville. By 1900 the extent of its wealth attracted a visit by the famed Butch Cassidy gang, who made an unauthorized bank withdrawal of $32,640.

Winnemucca is at the intersection of Interstate Highway 80, the Humboldt route, and US Highway 95, the north-south road along the western side of the state. North of this point US Highway 95 passes west of the Santa Rosa Mountains via the Quinn River Valley. The mountains are accessible from connecting roads on the east. Westward from the main highway other routes lead off into the lava beds and alkali flats of northwest Nevada.

Nevada route 8B skirts the east side of the mountains and heads into Paradise Valley from a point 22 miles north of Winnemucca. After another 18 miles the road arrives at the community that takes its name from the valley, where about one hundred fifty people live in a vale that really lives up to its name. Snug under the encircling arms of the Santa Rosa Range, the site is blessed with mountain creeks, gentle weather, and a whole spectrum of color on the slopes in late springtime. North out of the little valley the road loses its pavement, but some pioneer determination will get the explorer up to Hinkey Summit at 8,000 feet, or thereabouts. The trip is worth the extra effort, not just for the grand vista it opens to broad portions of northern Nevada, southern Oregon and Idaho, but also for the crowded communities of Indian paintbrush, purple lupine and tiny, wild yellow sunflowers in the meadows spreading away from the road. All this happens in summer, of course. Winter closes down the show, and the road.

The west side of the Santa Rosas is remote, unknown country, too. There's one little settlement—Orovada—on the route of US Highway 95 as it swings down through the broad Quinn River valley, that has some desert touches without quite being one. The valley has no trees, and for good reason: sometimes late in the season there is no water because, though the Quinn River heads in the Santa Rosa Mountains, it has a supply problem after a long, hot summer. When the river is doing its job, much of the water is diverted for irrigation of hay fields in the valley. Peter Skene Ogden, the Hudson's Bay trapper and explorer, would probably find the Quinn River country little changed from the early 1800s when he and his party followed the stream southward to the Humboldt.

The northwestern corner of Nevada produces desert and mountain vistas that seem to go on forever. The lower Quinn River, or what is left of it, winds through the flats west of its valley. The stream disappears somewhere in the vicinity of the Jackson Mountains, which define the eastern border of the long Black Rock Desert. That big alkali waste gave the early westward travelers second thoughts, and even today roads give the heart of the desert a wide berth. State Highway 140 south of Orovada swings north and west around its perimeter. Near the Oregon border is the lonely outpost of Denio, then the road heads farther west past the Pine Forest Range and other desert mountains that rise in wave after wave along the northwest fringes of this silent, empty land. Other routes, some gravel, on the western side complete the circle around it. The land is empty only from the human point of view. Among the abundant wildlife are antelope, who roam its eroded hills on a big refuge.

The only road that dares to probe into the desert for any distance is the dirt kind. It leads to the small Summit Lake Indian Reservation. Paiutes and Shoshones from Pyramid Lake to the south use the Summit Lake region for summer grazing of stock. While they live here, it is said, the Indians feel they experience a communion of spirit with the bleak canyons, mountains and flats on the desert's western fringes. It is a big land, and anyone who spends some time living in it and observing it cannot help but wonder if he will ever be satisfied living anywhere else on the face of the earth.

The desert and Mormon Range

State Capitol, Carson City

19

Black Rock Range

Reno

HAROLDS
HAROLDS CLUB
GARR NELSONS
HONKY TONK
STARRING
PATTY MALONEY
GINO ROSSI
WE'VE RESET OUR SLOTS NOW MORE WINNERS
NEVADA
COFFEE SHOP
CITY IN THE WORLD

Winnemucca Peak
(Following pages) Lake Tahoe

Cactus and Indian paintbrush

23

Jackson Mountains

Virginia City

Incline Village, Lake Tahoe

Tuscarora Mountains near Elko

Carson Sink

Ward Charcoal Ovens, near Ely

Charles Sheldon National Antelope Refuge

The Truckee River

Winnemucca Peak

Building in the ghost town of Osceola

Virginia City

36

Lake Tahoe

Winnemucca Peak

Walker Lake
(Following pages) Sunrise at Lake Tahoe

Pilot Peak

The Savage Mansion, Virginia City

43

The Castle

Pine Forest Range

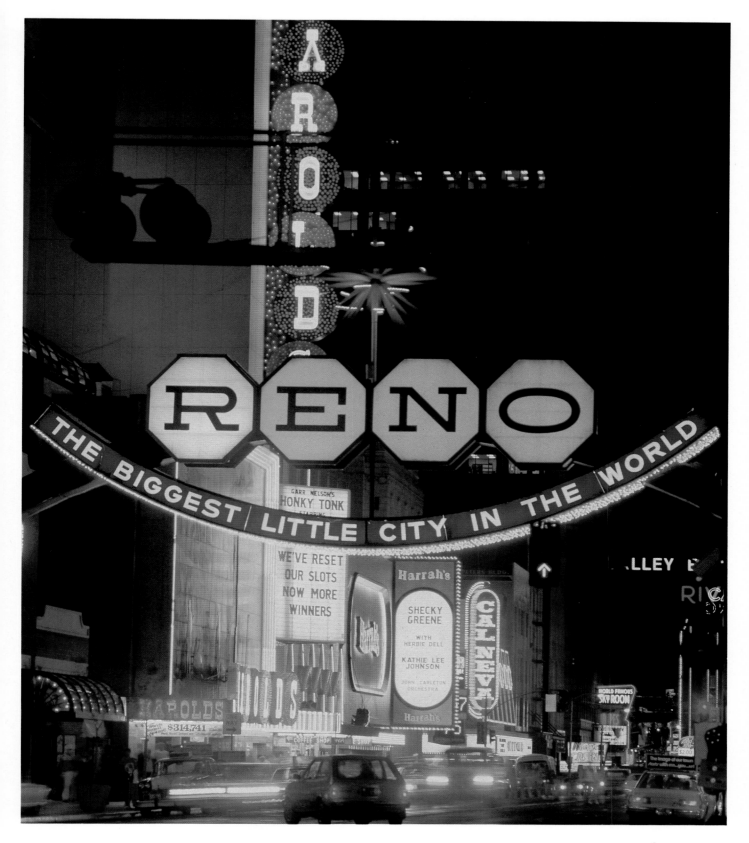

Reno

Pine Nut Mountain Range

Bloody Run Peak, near Winnemucca

Walker Lake

Santa Rosa Range

50

Mountain lake near Reno

Santa Rosa Range

Old gas pump in Currie

53

The Mackay Mansion, Virginia City
(Following pages) Lake Tahoe

Bloody Run Peak

55

Santa Rosa Range

Fourth Ward School, Virginia City

59

Santa Rosa Range

Virginia City

Pine Forest Range

Toiyable Forest

Ruby Mountain Range

The West
and the East

Western Nevada is where things got started. Some of the most colorful events in the opening of the West came about in the tight corner of western Nevada that gave birth to the state's first settlements and made certain that Nevada would have its own political identity.

The big town of these Sierra east-slope cities is Reno. But Reno was settled some years after the pioneer communities south of it in the Carson Valley. The Virginia Range of this valley proved to be a prodigious repository of gold and silver ores. These mountains were a "second chance" for the backwash of prospectors who had failed to make a good strike on the western Sierra slopes. The gold ore was an early attraction, but the more sensational discoveries were the rich veins of silver that were found a little later. Gold Hill was the first camp where exciting strikes were made. The district was established in Gold Canyon in 1859, when panning by a number of prospectors over the years began to pay off to the tune of $500 to $1,000 of gold a day.

While the gold miners were flocking in from the Mother Lode Country in California, and frantically staking claims over every square foot of the Virginia Range, there were only a few persons shrewd enough to surmise that the "worthless" black material that got in the way of the gold discovery might be valuable. Henry Comstock, whose name is synonymous with one of the world's richest silver strikes, and whose Comstock Lode was the basis of Virginia City, thought he had snookered a couple of prospectors out of some rich gold ore when he put in a claim for a share of their holding on the basis of prior discovery.

The population drawn by the gold and silver riches literally put Nevada on the map. Soon there were enough permanent residents in the Carson and Truckee river valleys for the federal government to create Nevada Territory out of the western portion of Utah Territory. Many of those first towns are still afloat and vibrant, including Carson City, the state capital, and Virginia City, still known as the Silver Heart of the Silver State. Gold Hill, Silver City and Genoa are alive, but not far removed from ghostly status.

Virginia City sits fairly secure these days over the tunnels that dig into its silver mountain. The silver bonanza city has been designated a National Historic Landmark. Carson City, from the start, had a second career laid out for it. It used to be the seat of Ormsby, the smallest county. Now it is a combined city-county, independent unto itself and capital of Nevada to boot.

Carson City was made the state capital in 1861, ten years after it began as a trading post on the Overland Trail to California. It aced out Genoa, the Territorial capital, in the process. Genoa, in its southern corner of the valley, still has something Carson City wasn't able to take from it—the title as oldest permanent Nevada town, settled around 1849. For a while Genoa fattened on the ebb tide of disappointed prospectors who had come up short in California and were stampeding back to Nevada on the news of rich ore discoveries. The travel and freight business across the Sierra gave Genoa its own version of a gold mine for a time. Nowadays the little town in the Sierra foothills, once so important in business and government, is barely visible, but is being saved from extinction as a colorful reminder of Nevada's role in the opening of the West.

Carson City has several advantages in addition to the early one of being handy to the trans-Sierra trails. The town is near the Carson River in a well-watered valley of the Sierra foothills. The site was surveyed in 1858 and the town began to take on substance in the next year when the pick-and-shovel armies were stampeding to the Comstock Lode. About that time it was named for Christopher (Kit) Carson, John C. Fremont's famous scout. The city was finally incorporated in 1875, eleven years after Nevada became a state. Carson City has a special reverence for Abraham Lincoln. He was the President who proclaimed Nevada the 36th state of the Union, of which Carson City became the capital.

The Carson City region shares the no-nonsense weather that prevails in a lot of Nevada: cold and dry in winter; warm and dry in summer. One big difference is the access to water that rolls off the high Sierra via the Carson and Truckee rivers and other streams. That quality made this mountain valley attractive to prospectors in the first place and must have contributed immensely to the longevity of the cluster of little old towns around Carson City, which by rights should have faded into the purple Nevada sunset by now.

There's Virginia City, of course, propped up by the lingering reputation of the fabulous Comstock. It's one of the bigger old towns where the ghosts of the Old West still have some substance. Other former big-time mining camps scattered around the hills and valleys are either ghost towns in the fullest sense or have ghostly appendages that still hang on into the present. Sutro, Fort Churchill, Ophir and Washoe City are examples of the former; Genoa, Gold Hill and Silver City belong to the latter group.

The "Biggest Little City in the World," or more modestly in western Nevada, is, as most of the world knows, Reno. Here is the biggest center of population in the state outside of Las Vegas. Counting next-door Sparks, that's about 140,000 persons. Reno's setting could hardly be surpassed. It's got the high wall of the Sierra on the west and the low, brown desert ranges to the east. The clear-running Truckee River bisects the town, which spreads out on the fertile river plain between the mountains. The Sierra-Lake Tahoe summer and winter recreation areas are easily accessible on US Highway 395. Weirdly beautiful Pyramid Lake is a short distance off to the north, and Walker, Nevada's other big lake, not much farther away on the southeast. The legendary gold and silver towns of the Virginia Range and Carson Valley are spread out nearby. Although Reno was not launched as a mining camp, the town's beginnings are related to the gold and silver strikes of the Virginia district. The Central Pacific railroad and the heavy Comstock freight business put Reno on the map in 1868. Before that the townsite on the green Truckee Meadows had been a haven and restorative for desert-weary travelers along the Overland Trail.

Reno became the seat of Washoe County by 1871, replacing Washoe City, one of today's "ghosts." It prospered on the Comstock production and by the time the mining activity leveled off in the eighties, the town was an established distribution point for a wide area of western Nevada. At the turn of the century, Reno got another boost from rich ore discoveries at Tonopah and Goldfield in south-central Nevada. The prosperity from that lasted ten years and pushed Reno, now a city, into a hefty population figure. After that boom subsided, Reno entrepreneurs attracted attention to the town by staging world championship heavyweight boxing matches. Jack Johnson, Jim Jeffries, Max Baer and Jack Dempsey all fought in the ring at Reno. This sort of event helped to give Reno world-wide repute, at least on the sports pages. When Nevada legalized gambling in 1931, Reno promoters gave it the full Madison Avenue treatment, along with publicity about Nevada's liberal divorce laws. So the town continued to prosper as more and more people found it a pleasant place to lose their money and their spouses all at once.

Reno has managed to preserve a respectable sample of its own past and that of some of the mining towns in the valley and around northern Nevada. There's a museum with household articles, tools and homemade musical instruments from the earliest days of several northern Nevada towns. The collection also includes bells from early Nevada churches, old photos and etchings, and Indian artifacts. Baroque elaboration is an aspect of the many splendid Victorian houses that can be found in the city, some of them moved to Reno from the hills of Virginia City.

The silver and gold kings knew how to spend money after they had made it. Some of their ornate homes survive to attest to that. One of the prize dwellings from that period is not in Reno, but south of town on US Highway 395. The Bowers Mansion is a legacy of the first Comstock millionaires, Lemuel and Ella Bowers. Looking like a transplanted Mediterranean villa, it has a broad sloping roof breached by a line of narrow dormers. The setting of swimming pools and a forecourt fountain in a nest of tall trees adds elegance to the exterior appearance. The Bowers' not only built their palace but furnished it lavishly with overpriced items acquired on a two-year European buying trip. The absorbing story of how the magnificent house was built and furnished has become a part of the Comstock heritage.

Reno's exceptional natural setting can be sampled in a 20-mile drive south of Virginia City, Gold Hill and Silver City in the mountains of the mining camps probed by State Highway 17. This is the Comstock Country where spectacular mountain-and-valley outlooks are part of Nevada's dramatic mining history. The road climbs gradually to 6,900 feet at the summit of the Virginia Range, and observation points along the way provide panoramic looks across the valleys in several directions. The mineral-rich slopes and deep chasms glint back at the winding road in a lavish range of bright or muted colors, depending on weather, haze, and distance. Blues, violets, reds, and gray-greens are spread over the tumbled miles, mingled with the bright green of cultivated fields in spring, and the dark green of the forests climbing up the steep flanks of the towering Sierras.

Nevada's three big lakes, particularly Tahoe, are almost in Reno's backyard. Pyramid is 33 miles away on the north. It is fed by the Truckee River, which flows out of Lake Tahoe, and by occasional freshets from the mountains and canyons around it. Pyramid is more than a lake—it is a whole geology lesson. The biggest remnant of ancient Lake Lahontan, it is surrounded by bare hills deeply dissected and folded, whose mineral soils glow pink and purple, or display streaks of other colors. Although the deep blue lake has no outlet, its depth is slowly diminishing.

John C. Fremont was the first of the explorers of the West to discover Pyramid Lake. Fremont, one of the trail blazers of the Nevada country, came down the western corridor from Oregon in 1843, into what is now long and lean Washoe County. He named Pyramid and Walker lakes, the latter in honor of Joseph Walker, his second in command, the former in honor of the bizarre tufa growths that sprout up from the lake waters and resemble pyramids in some cases. The island and shoreline formations of calcareous tufa, a porous limestone deposit, sometimes grow to monumental size and assume human-like shapes. Anaho Island, at the southern end of the 30-mile-long lake, is a bird refuge and pelican rookery. Great numbers of pelicans loiter around the mouth of the Truckee River at this end of the lake when the cui-ui, a rare species of fish, are running. Human fishermen prefer the lake's giant cutthroat trout, or landlocked salmon.

Nevada can only claim the eastern shore of Lake Tahoe, but that is no barrier to the flocks of recreationists who come to this Sierra paradise from Reno (and other places) at all times of the year. The huge, deep bowl of Tahoe lies halfway up the Sierra's east slope, with the surface at 6,225 feet. The lake bottom is as much as 1,776 feet below that. Tahoe and the slopes around it have become a northern Sierra sports empire for summer sailors and winter skiers. Even though many resorts line its shores on the Nevada side, there is still an unspoiled look and feel to this brilliant, 21-mile-long, blue-green mountain jewel.

Walker Lake, like Pyramid, has no outlet, but its large population of perch and trout don't seem to mind. Walker is 30 miles long, three to eight miles wide, and 1,000 feet at the point of maximum depth. Such a heavy store of water accounts for the lake's intense cobalt blue coloring. Lying well below the highway (US Highway 95) that skirts its western shore, the lake under the full sun resembles more of a narrow sea of molten metal than a body of water. The water levels of successive periods are marked by terraces on the lake shores.

Walker Lake owes most of its waters to Walker River, which comes in at the north end and, in turn, is beholden to the high Sierra slopes. In the fashion of great-looking lakes, Walker has chosen a setting that sets it off very well. The high Wassuk Range crowds the western shore, at some points forcing the roadway to take big bites out of the mountains in order to gain a decent foothold. The Wassuks are topped off by Mount Grant at the lower end of the lake. The peak is so accommodating to those who savor the loft lookout that it carries a road almost to the pinnacle. Once arrived at the 11,245-foot-high eyrie, the nearest reach to heaven in an endless stretch of wild Nevada, the view is like something conjured up in an extravagant and mystical fantasy. Just under the mountain is inky-blue Walker Lake. Rolling brown wrinkles to the east and south sort themselves out into separate mountain ranges, once their identity is determined from this great height. On the west the Sierra Nevada seems like a wall around the world, its summit drawing a snow-white line against the blue sky as far as the eye can see. Lost in all this grandeur, US Highway 95 wriggles and squirms its way through as if conscious of its own alien presence.

This kind of middle-earth spectacle is peculiar to much of central Nevada, all the way across the state. The region's only through routes, US Highway 50 and 6, sweep around its perimeter to the north and south, respectively. US Highway 50 is by all odds one of the finest long scenic highways anywhere. For a visual banquet early morning and late afternoon are the best times to be driving it. At those times the colors in the hills, mountains and desert valleys respond more vividly to the slanting light. The gullies and canyons just out of reach of the sun's touch are somber pools of deep blues and purples. Armadas of puffy clouds, blazing orange-red in the low light, reflect their glow onto the silent earth as they move around the sky. There may be other movement, too. On low meadows or high on the slopes, cattle and sheep are sometimes seen. Desert birds, hawks, buzzards and magpies soar into view high above, or patrol the roadsides, and eagles can be seen over the high ridges. Once in a while, where an occasional stream comes through, a line of cottonwoods and willows follows the bed, their green foliage or bare branches contrasting with the sage and scrub.

Here and there along the route are towns, or the remains of towns, that were once busy mining centers. Right in the middle of the state, US Highway 50 comes to Austin, one of the more successful and long lasting of the camps. Austin is very much alive today as a town center for remote mining and ranching communities of the area. Austin was another of the remarkable silver producers and the energizer for mining districts opened up over much of central and eastern Nevada, even while Virginia City's Comstock Lode was yielding up its unbelievable riches.

Austin is embedded more than 6,000 feet up in a canyon of the Toiyabe Range, a line of beautiful wooded mountains where wildlife is especially abundant. The Toiyabes and Shoshone mountains west of them furnish water for the Reese River and its fertile valley, 12 miles wide and 100 miles long.

Eureka is one of the old mining towns that have achieved an extended earthly life. It is 70 miles east of Austin and has a comparable permanent population of several hundred. Founded by Austin men in 1864, it developed into one of the many great boom towns that exploded all over the Nevada hills in the latter 1800s. Eureka was more sedate than the usual boisterous mining camp. The reason was the nature of its lead-silver ores, the first big find of this type in the country and the most resistant at that time to processing. Another factor was the frequency of lead poisoning from the bars of ore.

Hamilton is among the once-crowded towns that is no more, except for a few crumbling building foundations and sagging walls. In its day, from 1868 to about 1880, the camp in the White Pine Mountains southeast of Eureka was practically a metropolis. When the rush was in full gear at Hamilton, 25,000 potential millionaires were crowded into the district. The town was named for a promoter, appropriately, because everything about the place was frantically promoted, from its easy-to-get-at surface deposits to its high-priced town sites. The boom and the speculation ended when Hamilton's surface veins were found to be just that and little more. For a while Hamilton was the seat of new White Pine County, with a courthouse and other public and business buildings. By 1883 the rapid decline had begun, helped along by a series of fires that incinerated most of the buildings. In 1886 there were few remaining prospects or prospectors, so the county seat was moved to Ely, farther east.

Ely is now the biggest town in the east-central area. Founded as a gold-mining camp in 1868, it is built into a canyon high in the Egan Range. The community enjoys protection from the weather because of its steep canyon walls, and protection from a shortage of gold ore because the district turned out to be rich in copper deposits. The copper is harder to extract, but in comparatively inexhaustible supply.

Ely, its suburb East Ely, McGill and Ruth, four towns engaged in various ends of the copper business, are all clustered close together among the canyons, hills, and valleys of the spectacular mountain wilderness of eastern Nevada. McGill is the farthest north, hard by the tall Schell Creek Range. Nevada's east-side highway, US Highway 93, comes down from the north in a straight shot through Steptoe Valley, a long, wide, level basin whose distant horizon seems to the traveler to fall off the edge of the earth.

To say Ruth is a big hole in the ground would be in no way derogatory. The town is the site of the Copper Pit, formerly one of the world's largest open pit copper mines, a terraced hole of immense depth and yawning breadth. Nature, however, went the other way when she created this wild country where US Highway 50, 6, and 93 come together. Some of Nevada's tallest mountains are in the neighborhood. Wheeler Peak in the Snake Range is one, topping off at 13,061 feet, second highest point in the state. The mountain and its environs have been designated the Wheeler Peak Scenic Area. The preserve has its own version of a hole in the ground, one that came with the territory. This is Lehman Caves National Monument, spread out among the evergreen forests and canyons of the high Snake Range. The caves were discovered by accident in the 1870s when a logger named Abe Lehman and his anonymous horse fell through the surface into them as they were hauling logs down the mountainside. Up to that time the caverns had no entrance, and so they were very clean. The beautiful limestone formations in them have an exceptional purity and range of color. A complication of corridors and tunnels connects vast chambers where floor-to-ceiling limestone columns may be as much as 60 feet high.

A hole in the ground may seem an odd stopping place for a commentary on Nevada's scenic resources. On the other hand, closing with the Lehman Caves underlines the marvelous variety of nature's art, Nevada-style. More and more people are being attracted to Nevada; that is affirmed by the 1980 Census findings proclaiming it the fastest-growing state. The new Nevadans are not all going to Las Vegas and Reno, either. Some of the 20th-century settlers are indeed discovering a Nevada that is more than gaming tables and glossy entertainments. In the remote wilds of Nevada's mountains, valleys and deserts are the strengths of a state that seems destined for a large role in our nation's 21st century.

Beautiful America Publishing Company

The nation's foremost publisher of quality color photography

Current Books

Alaska	Maryland	Oregon Vol. II
Arizona	Massachusetts	Oregon Coast
Boston	Michigan	Oregon Country
British Columbia	Michigan Vol. II	Pacific Coast
California	Minnesota	Pennsylvania
California Vol. II	Missouri	Pittsburgh
California Coast	Montana	San Diego
California Desert	Montana Vol. II	San Francisco
California Missions	Monterey Peninsula	San Juan Islands
California Mountains	Mormon	Seattle
Chicago	Mt. Hood (Oregon)	Tennessee
Colorado	Nevada	Texas
Dallas	New Jersey	Utah
Delaware	New Mexico	Utah Country
Denver	New York	Vancouver U.S.A.
Florida	New York City	Vermont
Georgia	Northern California	Virginia
Hawaii	Northern California Vol. II	Volcano Mt. St. Helens
Idaho	North Carolina	Washington
Illinois	North Idaho	Washington Vol. II
Indiana	Ohio	Washington, D.C.
Kentucky	Oklahoma	Wisconsin
Las Vegas	Orange County	Wyoming
Los Angeles, 200 Years	Oregon	Yosemite National Park

Forthcoming Books

Alabama	Kauai	Oahu
Arkansas	Maine	Phoenix
Baltimore	Maui	Rhode Island
Connecticut	Mississippi	Rocky Mountains
Detroit	New England	South Carolina
The Great Lakes	New Hampshire	South Dakota
Houston	North Dakota	West Virginia
Kansas		

Large Format, Hardbound Books

Beautiful America	Beauty of Washington	Lewis & Clark Country
Beauty of California	Glory of Nature's Form	Western Impressions
Beauty of Oregon	Volcanoes of the West	

For a complete product catalog, send $1.00.
Beautiful America Publishing Company
P.O. Box 608
Beaverton, Oregon 97075